Apple Cider Days

by Robert R. O'Brien

MODERN CURRICULUM PRESS

Pearson Learning Group

It is mid-winter. Snow blankets the ground. The apple trees are bare of leaves. Apples still hang on some of the branches, too high for deer to eat.

It doesn't seem like the time to think about apple blossoms, ripening fruit, and smooth, sweet apple cider. But the men and women trudging through the snow with chainsaws and shears are thinking about those very things.

They are pruning apple trees in their orchard. Pruning goes on from January through March. This is the time of year to make sure that the trees have the best shape for growing apples.

There are two reasons to prune the trees. First, it is important to remove small branches. These would take water and food from the apples. These branches are called water buds, or "suckers," because they suck water from the branches where apples are growing.

The other reason to remove branches is to let more light into the trees. If the branches are too thick, light can't get in. Without lots of light, the middle of a tree won't keep growing. The apples also react to more light by getting more color.

The old rule that pruners use is "Prune so you can throw a cat through the tree." Of course, they would never really throw a cat through a tree! But the idea is to prune so there is plenty of space around each branch.

In April and May, the growers get busy
spreading fertilizer through the orchard. Fertilizer is
like food for trees. It gives them the nutrients they
need to grow strong, healthy apples.

Early spring is also the time when the apple
growers spray chemicals. These chemicals keep
bugs and diseases off the trees. Then they use weed
killers between the rows of trees. The weed killers
make sure that nutrients go to the trees, not
to weeds.

In late May, the apple trees blossom. This is a tricky time. In the North, snow and frost may still come. And that can damage blossoms.

But even if it does get cold, the nectar from the blossoms will attract bumblebees. Apple growers in Maine say, "Bumblebees will fly with snowshoes on." That means that cold weather that would keep other bees in the hive has no effect on bumblebees.

On warmer days, wasps, hornets, and honeybees also help the tree farmers. Like the bumblebees, they spread pollen as they collect nectar from the pink and white blossoms.

The apple petals fall in early June. Then the apple growers have tight schedules to follow. For exactly seven to fourteen days after blossoms fall, apple producers can spray a chemical that thins the apples out.

Thinning means killing off most of the apple buds. Each apple blossom makes one bud. The blossoms grow in clusters of five. Each cluster can grow five apples. But if you remove most of the buds in a cluster, then instead of five very small apples, you get one large apple. All of the nutrients in that little branch will go into one apple. And that's what apple producers want.

Every blossom cluster has a "king bloom." The king bloom is one blossom that opens sooner than the others. It might open eight, or twelve, or twenty-four hours before the rest. That shows it's stronger. The apple grower kills the weaker, unopened buds, leaving the strongest bud to make a strong apple.

The rest of July and August are used for hand thinning. That means that each tree gets checked. If there are too many apples on a twig, the smallest ones get pulled off.

In September the apple harvest begins. In small orchards, every apple is hand-picked. This protects the apples from getting bruised.

Next the condition of the apples is checked. They are sorted, or "graded," by size, color, shape, and number of blemishes. Fancy apples, with no blemishes, are sold as eating or cooking apples. Some apples are sound, but have small blemishes. This condition makes them good candidates for cider.

Apples of different varieties—Northern Spy, Golden Delicious, Macintosh, Cortland—are mixed to make cider. A mixture of apple types makes a tastier drink. Different cider producers use different mixtures. They keep their recipes secret.

Cider makers fill a wooden bin with about fifteen bushels of apples. The bin is brought to a grinder, which is used to extract juice from the apples. The apples are dumped into a grinder. The grinder is a drum with stainless steel teeth. It chews the apples, turning them into a chunky mush.

The mush then goes into the press mold. The mold is a wood frame with a fine mesh. It is covered with a cloth. The apple mush is put in the cloth. Then the sides of the cloth are folded over the mush to cover it. A wooden rack is placed over that, and then another stack is started. When the stack is about two-feet tall, the press starts to push down on the top rack.

The press pushes with strength equal to 1,800 pounds. The juice from the apple mush gets squeezed out into a stainless steel basin. Stainless steel is used because it will not react with the cider to change the taste. One bushel of apples makes three to four gallons of cider.

When the basin is full, the cider is pumped into
a stainless steel refrigerator tank for storage. The
cider stays there until it is sold. It is then drained,
one gallon at a time, into plastic jugs.

The jugs are brought to market to sell. Many
small orchards also have their own stores where they
sell apples, cider, and other apple products.

Harvest season lasts through mid-October. After the apples are harvested they are kept in storage in a refrigerated warehouse. That way, they stay in fresh condition longer. Some may be used to make more cider, later in the year.

Cider producers keep making fresh cider through December. In January, they start all over again, pruning trees for the next fall's apple crop.

It's hard work. But after a long day of raking leaves or a hot game of touch football, there is nothing like the sweet, tangy taste of freshly-squeezed cider.